47 HOW THE FUCK DID THAT HAPPEN

47
oh
fuckity
fuck

Today
Is the
FUCKING
Awesome
Birthday

YOU FUCKIN' GOT THIS

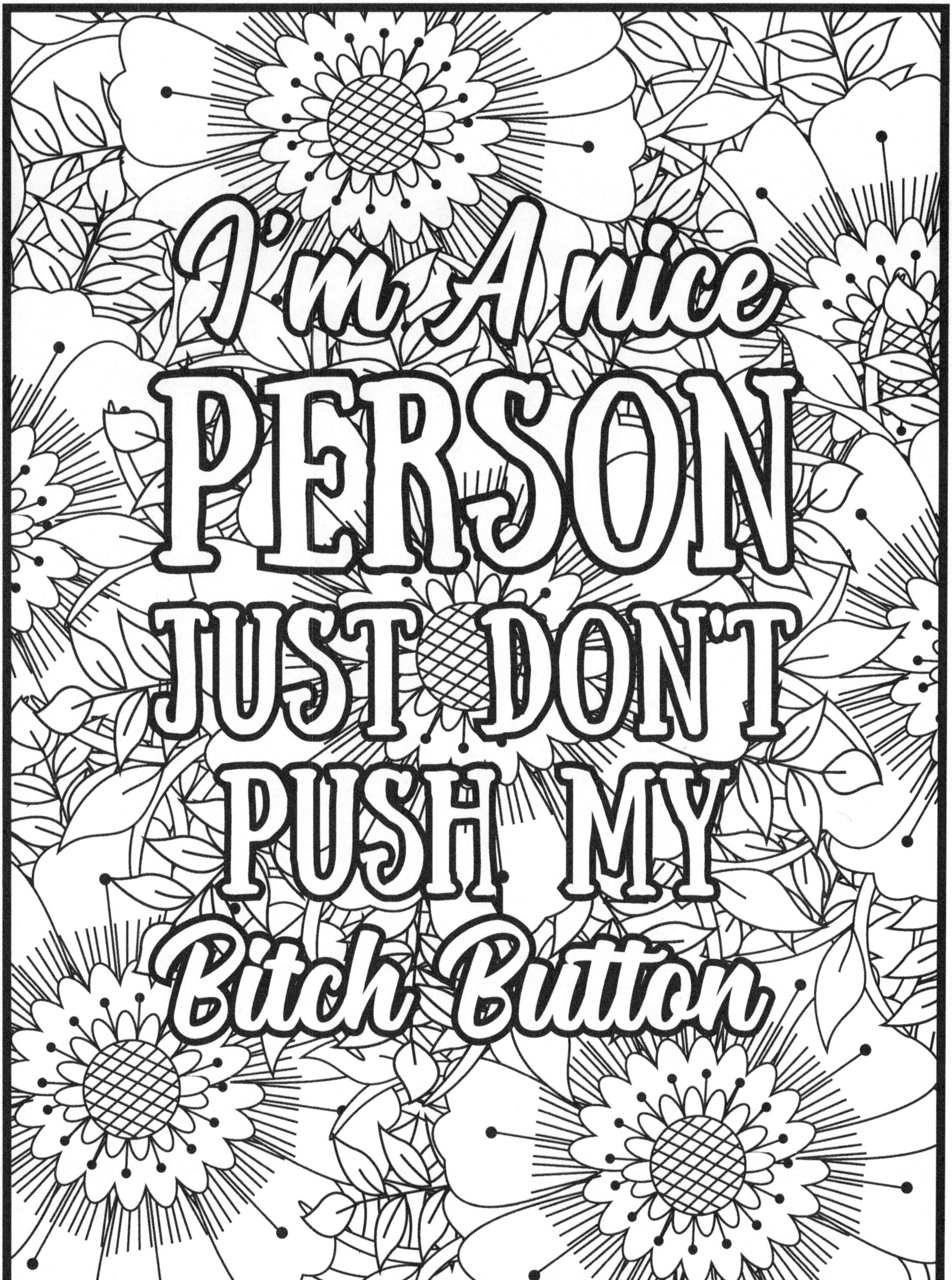
I'm A nice
PERSON
JUST DON'T
PUSH MY
Bitch Button

I can &
I FUCKING
Will

fucking
Awesome
Birthday

be Happy
EVERY
damn
DAY!

Holly
FUCK
I AM 47

You Are
AMAZING
As Fuck

I'm A Kind
OF A
FUCKING
GREAT
Deal

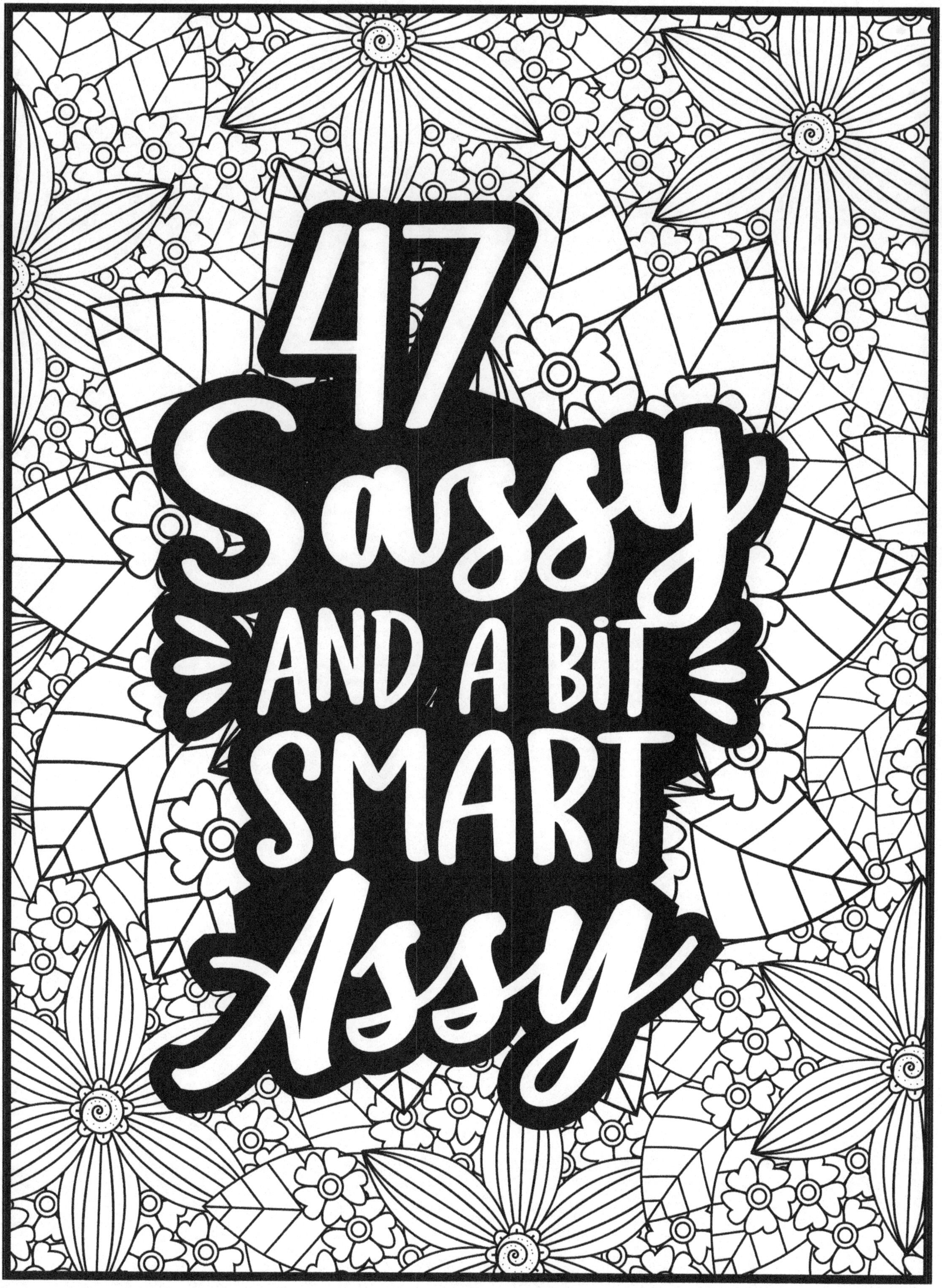
47
Sassy
AND A BIT
SMART
Assy

Hey, you're Fucking Great

SMILE MORE.
WORRY
FUCKING
LESS!

I'm
46+

Fuck
Perfect

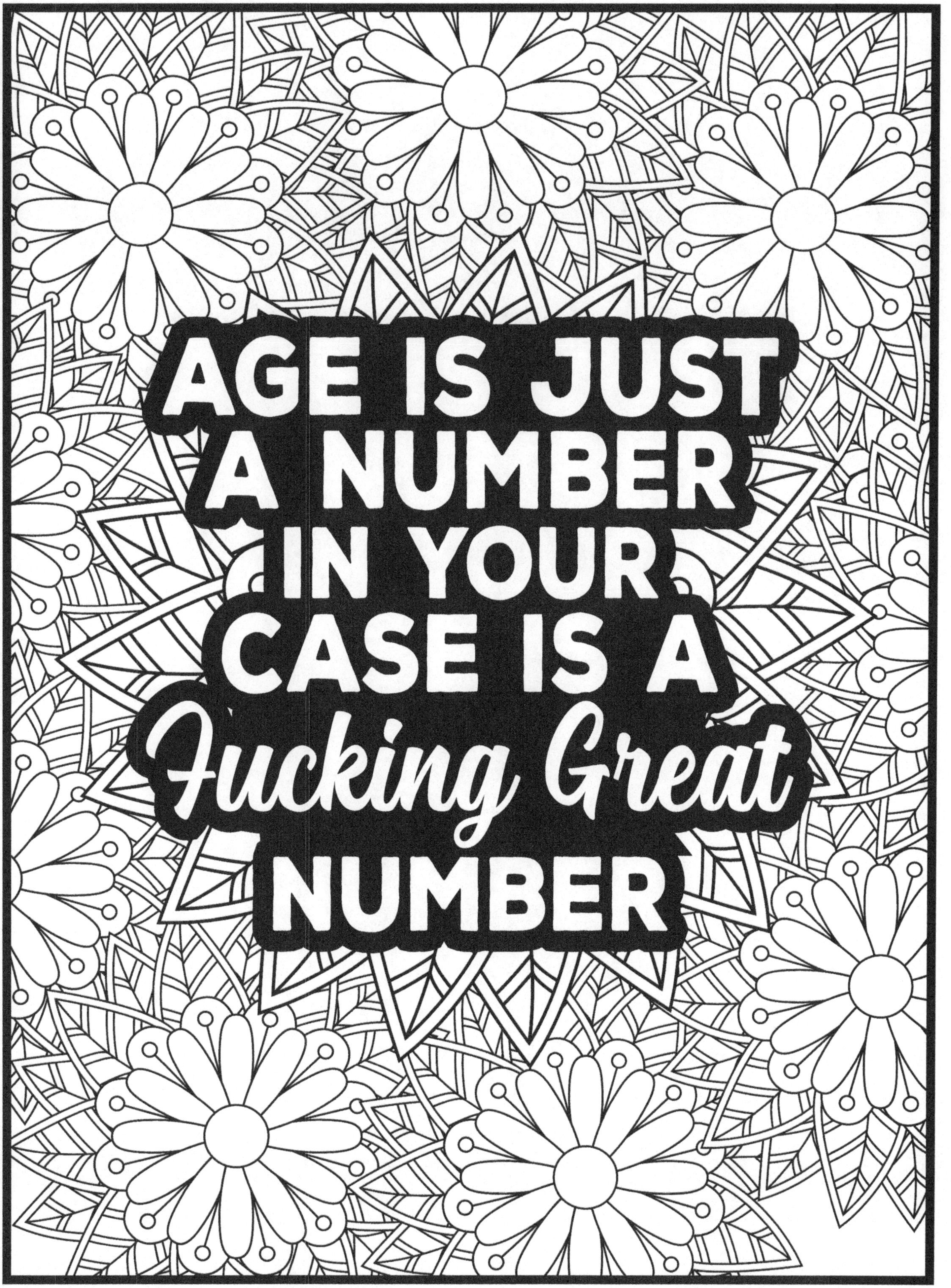
AGE IS JUST
A NUMBER
IN YOUR
CASE IS A
Fucking Great
NUMBER

Too Calm
TO GIVE A
Damn

keep Calm
AND BE
fucking
FABULOUS
AT 47

IT TOOK ME
47 YEARS
TO LOOK
THIS GOOD

Calm The
Fuck
Down

TURNING
47 LIKE:
I CAN FEEL
MYSELF
ROTTING.

WAKE UP
AND BE
FUCKING
Awesome
EVERYDAY

You Are
A FUCKING
47
Year Old
Rock
NOW

Spread Love
EVERYWHERE
YOU FUCKING
GO

Fucks
&
cheers
to 47
Years

YOU ARE
Awesome As
FUCK

You Are
A FUCKING
Legend

be happy
IT DRIVES
ASSHOLES
Crazy

Cheer
The
Fuck
Up

TAKE NO
SHITS.
GIVE NO
FUCKS.

I Gave
ZeRO
FUCKS
Today

Let That
Shit
go

WHY DON'T
You Fucking
Do it

WAKE UP.
KICK SOME
FUCKING ASS.
REPEAT.

You Are
Fucking
HANDSOME
At the age of
47

THE BEST
is yet to
FUCKING
COME

Fuck
Aging

Fuck
Off

Test Your Colors

Made in the USA
Las Vegas, NV
09 October 2024

96533828R00046